HAL•LEONARD

JAZZ PLAY ALONG®

Book and CD for B♭, E♭, C and Bass Clef Instruments

Volume **70**

Produced by Mark Taylor
Arranged by Jim Roberts

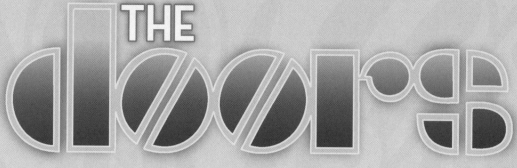

THE **Doors**

Cover photo: Photofest
ISBN 13: 978-1-4234-2387-4

T0066118

HAL•LEONARD®
CORPORATION

7777 W. BLUEMOUND RD. P.O. BOX 13819 MILWAUKEE, WI 53213

Visit Hal Leonard Online at
www.halleonard.com

The Doors

Volume 70

Produced by Mark Taylor
Arranged by Jim Roberts

Featured Players:

Graham Breedlove-Trumpet
John Desalme-Saxophones
Tony Nalker-Piano
Jim Roberts-Bass
Steve Fidyk-Drums

Recorded at Bias Studios, Springfield, Virginia
Bob Dawson, Engineer

HOW TO USE THE CD:

Each song has two tracks:

1) Split Track/Melody

Woodwind, Brass, Keyboard, and **Mallet Players** can use this track as a learning tool for melody style and inflection.

Bass Players can learn and perform with this track – Remove the recorded bass track by turning down the volume on the LEFT channel.

Keyboard and **Guitar Players** can learn and perform with this track – remove the recorded piano part by turning down the volume on the RIGHT channel.

2) Full Stereo Track

Soloists or **Groups** can learn and perform with this accompaniment track with the RHYTHM SECTION only.

CD
❶ : SPLIT TRACK/MELODY
❷ : FULL STEREO TRACK

BREAK ON THROUGH
TO THE OTHER SIDE

WORDS AND MUSIC BY
THE DOORS

C VERSION

THE END

CD
❸ : SPLIT TRACK/MELODY
❹ : FULL STEREO TRACK

WORDS AND MUSIC BY
THE DOORS

C VERSION

CD
5 : SPLIT TRACK/MELODY
6 : FULL STEREO TRACK

C VERSION

HELLO, I LOVE YOU
(WON'T YOU TELL ME YOUR NAME?)

WORDS AND MUSIC BY
THE DOORS

L.A. WOMAN

WORDS AND MUSIC BY
THE DOORS

C VERSION

LIGHT MY FIRE

WORDS AND MUSIC BY
THE DOORS

LOVE ME TWO TIMES

CD
11: SPLIT TRACK/MELODY
12: FULL STEREO TRACK

WORDS AND MUSIC BY
THE DOORS

C VERSION

SOLOS (3 CHORUSES)

D.S. AL FINE
WITH REPEAT

RIDERS ON THE STORM

CD
15 : SPLIT TRACK/MELODY
16 : FULL STEREO TRACK

WORDS AND MUSIC BY
THE DOORS

C VERSION

PEOPLE ARE STRANGE

WORDS AND MUSIC BY
THE DOORS

TOUCH ME

WORDS AND MUSIC BY
THE DOORS

CD

19 : SPLIT TRACK/MELODY

20 : FULL STEREO TRACK

C VERSION

CD

ROADHOUSE BLUES

WORDS AND MUSIC BY
THE DOORS

C VERSION

MEDIUM SHUFFLE

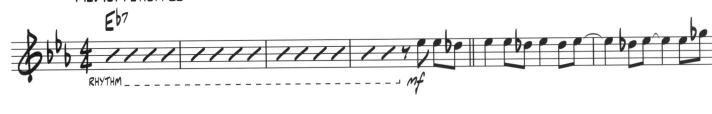

THE END

WORDS AND MUSIC BY
THE DOORS

BREAK ON THROUGH
TO THE OTHER SIDE

WORDS AND MUSIC BY
THE DOORS

HELLO, I LOVE YOU
(WON'T YOU TELL ME YOUR NAME?)

WORDS AND MUSIC BY
THE DOORS

Bb VERSION

MEDIUM SOUL JAZZ

L.A. WOMAN

WORDS AND MUSIC BY
THE DOORS

LIGHT MY FIRE

WORDS AND MUSIC BY
THE DOORS

LOVE ME TWO TIMES

WORDS AND MUSIC BY
THE DOORS

CD
11 : SPLIT TRACK/MELODY
12 : FULL STEREO TRACK

Bb VERSION MEDIUM SHUFFLE

RIDERS ON THE STORM

WORDS AND MUSIC BY
THE DOORS

Bb VERSION

ROADHOUSE BLUES

WORDS AND MUSIC BY
THE DOORS

PEOPLE ARE STRANGE

WORDS AND MUSIC BY
THE DOORS

TOUCH ME

CD
◆19 : SPLIT TRACK/MELODY
◆20 : FULL STEREO TRACK

WORDS AND MUSIC BY
THE DOORS

Bb VERSION

BREAK ON THROUGH TO THE OTHER SIDE

WORDS AND MUSIC BY
THE DOORS

THE END

WORDS AND MUSIC BY
THE DOORS

E♭ VERSION

HELLO, I LOVE YOU
(WON'T YOU TELL ME YOUR NAME?)

WORDS AND MUSIC BY
THE DOORS

L.A. WOMAN

CD
◆7 : SPLIT TRACK/MELODY
◆8 : FULL STEREO TRACK

WORDS AND MUSIC BY
THE DOORS

LIGHT MY FIRE

WORDS AND MUSIC BY
THE DOORS

LOVE ME TWO TIMES

WORDS AND MUSIC BY
THE DOORS

RIDERS ON THE STORM

WORDS AND MUSIC BY
THE DOORS

PEOPLE ARE STRANGE

WORDS AND MUSIC BY
THE DOORS

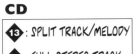

CD
⑬ : SPLIT TRACK/MELODY
⑭ : FULL STEREO TRACK

E♭ VERSION

TOUCH ME

WORDS AND MUSIC BY
THE DOORS

Eb VERSION

ROADHOUSE BLUES

WORDS AND MUSIC BY
THE DOORS

E♭ VERSION

THE END

WORDS AND MUSIC BY
THE DOORS

BREAK ON THROUGH TO THE OTHER SIDE

CD
5 : SPLIT TRACK/MELODY
6 : FULL STEREO TRACK

HELLO, I LOVE YOU
(WON'T YOU TELL ME YOUR NAME?)

WORDS AND MUSIC BY
THE DOORS

L.A. WOMAN

WORDS AND MUSIC BY
THE DOORS

LIGHT MY FIRE

WORDS AND MUSIC BY
THE DOORS

Love Me Two Times

WORDS AND MUSIC BY
THE DOORS

CD
⌂ : SPLIT TRACK/MELODY
12 : FULL STEREO TRACK

𝄢: C VERSION

PEOPLE ARE STRANGE

WORDS AND MUSIC BY
THE DOORS

CD
15 : SPLIT TRACK/MELODY
16 : FULL STEREO TRACK

RIDERS ON THE STORM

WORDS AND MUSIC BY
THE DOORS

ROADHOUSE BLUES

WORDS AND MUSIC BY
THE DOORS

TOUCH ME

WORDS AND MUSIC BY
THE DOORS